50 Low-Fat Dish Recipes for Home

By: Kelly Johnson

Table of Contents

- Grilled Chicken Breast with Lemon and Herbs
- Steamed Fish with Ginger and Soy Sauce
- Turkey and Vegetable Stir-Fry
- Baked Cod with Tomato and Basil
- Vegetable and Bean Chili
- Lemon Garlic Shrimp Skewers
- Baked Chicken Parmesan
- Roasted Vegetable Salad with Balsamic Vinaigrette
- Turkey Meatball Soup with Vegetables
- Grilled Salmon with Dill and Lemon
- Spaghetti Squash Primavera
- Quinoa Salad with Chickpeas and Cucumber
- Turkey Taco Lettuce Wraps
- Veggie-packed Minestrone Soup
- Lemon Herb Tilapia
- Ratatouille
- Turkey and Sweet Potato Hash
- Grilled Vegetable Skewers
- Lentil Soup with Spinach and Tomatoes
- Baked Chicken Tenders with Honey Mustard Sauce
- Tofu Stir-Fry with Broccoli and Bell Peppers
- Cauliflower Fried Rice
- Lemon Herb Grilled Chicken
- Greek Salad with Grilled Chicken
- Baked Eggplant Parmesan
- Shrimp and Vegetable Stir-Fry with Brown Rice
- Turkey and Black Bean Chili
- Baked Zucchini Fries
- Asian-style Tofu Lettuce Wraps
- Mediterranean Chickpea Salad
- Lemon Garlic Baked Cod
- Turkey and Spinach Stuffed Bell Peppers
- Baked Falafel with Tzatziki Sauce
- Grilled Portobello Mushrooms with Balsamic Glaze
- Spicy Thai Coconut Curry with Vegetables

- Broccoli and Cheddar Stuffed Chicken Breast
- Turkey and Vegetable Meatloaf
- Cauliflower and Chickpea Curry
- Lemon Garlic Roasted Chicken Thighs
- Baked Salmon with Dill Sauce
- Mediterranean Quinoa Salad
- Tofu and Vegetable Stir-Fry with Peanut Sauce
- Baked Cod with Herbed Crust
- Turkey and White Bean Soup
- Grilled Vegetable Quesadillas
- Lemon Herb Baked Tilapia
- Lentil and Vegetable Shepherd's Pie
- Baked Chicken with Rosemary and Garlic
- Spaghetti Squash with Marinara Sauce
- Turkey and Vegetable Skillet Hash

Grilled Chicken Breast with Lemon and Herbs

Ingredients:

- 4 boneless, skinless chicken breasts
- 2 tablespoons olive oil
- 2 cloves garlic, minced
- 2 teaspoons fresh lemon zest
- 2 tablespoons fresh lemon juice
- 1 tablespoon chopped fresh herbs (such as rosemary, thyme, or parsley)
- Salt and pepper to taste

Instructions:

1. Preheat your grill to medium-high heat.
2. In a small bowl, whisk together the olive oil, minced garlic, lemon zest, lemon juice, chopped herbs, salt, and pepper to make the marinade.
3. Place the chicken breasts in a shallow dish or resealable plastic bag. Pour the marinade over the chicken, making sure it's well coated. Marinate in the refrigerator for at least 30 minutes, or up to 4 hours for maximum flavor.
4. Remove the chicken from the marinade and discard any excess marinade.
5. Grill the chicken breasts for about 6-8 minutes per side, or until they are cooked through and have reached an internal temperature of 165°F (75°C). Cooking time may vary depending on the thickness of the chicken breasts.
6. Once cooked, remove the chicken from the grill and let it rest for a few minutes before serving.
7. Serve the grilled chicken breasts with your favorite side dishes, such as grilled vegetables, rice, or a fresh salad.
8. Enjoy your delicious Grilled Chicken Breast with Lemon and Herbs!

Steamed Fish with Ginger and Soy Sauce

Ingredients:

- 4 fish fillets (such as tilapia, cod, or sea bass)
- 2 tablespoons soy sauce
- 2 tablespoons rice vinegar
- 1 tablespoon sesame oil
- 1 tablespoon fresh ginger, grated
- 2 cloves garlic, minced
- 1 tablespoon honey or brown sugar
- 2 green onions, thinly sliced
- Salt and pepper to taste
- Sesame seeds and chopped cilantro for garnish (optional)

Instructions:

1. Rinse the fish fillets under cold water and pat them dry with paper towels. Season both sides of the fillets with salt and pepper.
2. In a small bowl, whisk together the soy sauce, rice vinegar, sesame oil, grated ginger, minced garlic, and honey or brown sugar until well combined.
3. Place the fish fillets in a shallow dish or on a plate large enough to hold them in a single layer. Pour the soy sauce mixture over the fish, making sure to coat each fillet evenly. Allow the fish to marinate for about 15-30 minutes in the refrigerator.
4. While the fish is marinating, prepare your steamer. If you don't have a steamer, you can use a large pot with a steaming rack or basket.
5. Once the fish has finished marinating, arrange the fillets in the steamer basket, leaving some space between each fillet for steam to circulate.
6. Steam the fish over simmering water for about 8-10 minutes, or until the fish is opaque and flakes easily with a fork. Cooking time may vary depending on the thickness of the fillets.
7. Carefully remove the steamed fish from the steamer and transfer them to a serving platter.
8. Garnish the fish with sliced green onions, sesame seeds, and chopped cilantro, if desired.
9. Serve the Steamed Fish with Ginger and Soy Sauce immediately, accompanied by steamed rice or your favorite side dishes.

10. Enjoy your delicious and healthy steamed fish dish!

Turkey and Vegetable Stir-Fry

Ingredients:

- 500g turkey breast, thinly sliced
- 2 tablespoons soy sauce
- 1 tablespoon oyster sauce
- 1 tablespoon rice vinegar
- 1 tablespoon hoisin sauce
- 1 tablespoon sesame oil
- 2 tablespoons vegetable oil, divided
- 2 cloves garlic, minced
- 1-inch piece of ginger, grated
- 1 onion, thinly sliced
- 2 bell peppers (any color), thinly sliced
- 1 cup broccoli florets
- 1 carrot, julienned
- Salt and pepper to taste
- Cooked rice or noodles, for serving
- Sesame seeds and chopped green onions for garnish (optional)

Instructions:

1. In a bowl, combine the soy sauce, oyster sauce, rice vinegar, hoisin sauce, and sesame oil. Stir well to combine. This will be your stir-fry sauce.
2. Heat 1 tablespoon of vegetable oil in a large skillet or wok over medium-high heat.
3. Add the sliced turkey breast to the skillet and stir-fry for 4-5 minutes until cooked through. Remove the turkey from the skillet and set aside.
4. In the same skillet, heat the remaining tablespoon of vegetable oil over medium-high heat.
5. Add the minced garlic and grated ginger to the skillet, and stir-fry for 1 minute until fragrant.
6. Add the sliced onion, bell peppers, broccoli florets, and julienned carrot to the skillet. Stir-fry for 5-6 minutes until the vegetables are tender-crisp.
7. Return the cooked turkey to the skillet with the vegetables.

8. Pour the stir-fry sauce over the turkey and vegetables. Stir well to coat everything evenly in the sauce.
9. Cook for another 2-3 minutes, stirring constantly, until everything is heated through and well combined.
10. Season with salt and pepper to taste.
11. Remove the skillet from the heat.
12. Serve the Turkey and Vegetable Stir-Fry hot over cooked rice or noodles.
13. Garnish with sesame seeds and chopped green onions, if desired.

Enjoy your delicious and nutritious Turkey and Vegetable Stir-Fry!

Baked Cod with Tomato and Basil

Ingredients:

- 4 cod fillets (about 6 ounces each)
- 2 tablespoons olive oil
- 2 cloves garlic, minced
- 1 can (14 ounces) diced tomatoes, drained
- 1/4 cup chopped fresh basil leaves
- 1 tablespoon lemon juice
- Salt and pepper to taste
- Lemon wedges for serving
- Fresh basil leaves for garnish (optional)

Instructions:

1. Preheat your oven to 375°F (190°C).
2. Pat the cod fillets dry with paper towels and place them in a baking dish that has been lightly greased with olive oil.
3. In a small skillet, heat the olive oil over medium heat. Add the minced garlic and sauté for 1-2 minutes until fragrant.
4. Add the diced tomatoes to the skillet and cook for another 2-3 minutes, stirring occasionally, until heated through.
5. Remove the skillet from the heat and stir in the chopped fresh basil leaves and lemon juice. Season with salt and pepper to taste.
6. Spoon the tomato and basil mixture over the cod fillets, spreading it evenly.
7. Cover the baking dish with aluminum foil and bake in the preheated oven for 15-20 minutes, or until the fish is opaque and flakes easily with a fork.
8. Once the cod is cooked through, remove the foil from the baking dish and switch the oven to broil.
9. Broil the cod for an additional 2-3 minutes, or until the top is lightly browned and caramelized.
10. Remove the cod from the oven and let it rest for a few minutes before serving.
11. Serve the Baked Cod with Tomato and Basil hot, garnished with fresh basil leaves and lemon wedges.

Enjoy your delicious and healthy Baked Cod with Tomato and Basil!

Vegetable and Bean Chili

Ingredients:

- 2 tablespoons olive oil
- 1 onion, diced
- 3 cloves garlic, minced
- 1 bell pepper, diced
- 2 carrots, diced
- 2 stalks celery, diced
- 1 zucchini, diced
- 1 cup corn kernels (fresh or frozen)
- 1 can (15 ounces) kidney beans, drained and rinsed
- 1 can (15 ounces) black beans, drained and rinsed
- 1 can (28 ounces) diced tomatoes
- 1 cup vegetable broth or water
- 2 tablespoons tomato paste
- 2 teaspoons chili powder
- 1 teaspoon ground cumin
- 1 teaspoon paprika
- 1/2 teaspoon dried oregano
- Salt and pepper to taste
- Fresh cilantro or parsley for garnish (optional)
- Sour cream or Greek yogurt for serving (optional)
- Shredded cheese for serving (optional)
- Sliced jalapeños for serving (optional)

Instructions:

1. Heat olive oil in a large pot or Dutch oven over medium heat.
2. Add diced onion to the pot and sauté for 3-4 minutes until translucent.
3. Add minced garlic to the pot and sauté for another 1-2 minutes until fragrant.
4. Add diced bell pepper, carrots, celery, and zucchini to the pot. Cook for 5-6 minutes until the vegetables start to soften.
5. Stir in corn kernels, kidney beans, black beans, diced tomatoes, vegetable broth (or water), and tomato paste.

6. Season the chili with chili powder, ground cumin, paprika, dried oregano, salt, and pepper. Stir well to combine.
7. Bring the chili to a simmer, then reduce the heat to low. Cover and let it simmer for 20-25 minutes, stirring occasionally, until the vegetables are tender and the flavors are well blended.
8. Taste the chili and adjust the seasoning if needed.
9. Serve the Vegetable and Bean Chili hot, garnished with fresh cilantro or parsley, a dollop of sour cream or Greek yogurt, shredded cheese, and sliced jalapeños if desired.
10. Enjoy this delicious and comforting Vegetable and Bean Chili on its own or with your favorite toppings!

Feel free to customize this chili recipe by adding other vegetables or spices according to your taste preferences.

Lemon Garlic Shrimp Skewers

Ingredients:

- 500g large shrimp, peeled and deveined
- 2 tablespoons olive oil
- 3 cloves garlic, minced
- Zest of 1 lemon
- Juice of 1 lemon
- 1 teaspoon paprika
- 1 teaspoon dried oregano
- Salt and pepper to taste
- Lemon wedges for serving
- Chopped fresh parsley for garnish (optional)

Instructions:

1. If you're using wooden skewers, soak them in water for about 30 minutes to prevent them from burning on the grill.
2. In a mixing bowl, combine olive oil, minced garlic, lemon zest, lemon juice, paprika, dried oregano, salt, and pepper. Mix well to create the marinade.
3. Add the peeled and deveined shrimp to the marinade, making sure they are well coated. Cover the bowl and refrigerate for at least 30 minutes to allow the flavors to meld.
4. Preheat your grill to medium-high heat.
5. Thread the marinated shrimp onto skewers, making sure to leave a little space between each shrimp.
6. Place the shrimp skewers on the preheated grill and cook for 2-3 minutes per side, or until the shrimp are pink and opaque.
7. Once the shrimp are cooked through, remove them from the grill and transfer them to a serving platter.
8. Garnish the Lemon Garlic Shrimp Skewers with chopped fresh parsley, if desired, and serve hot with lemon wedges on the side.
9. Enjoy your flavorful and aromatic Lemon Garlic Shrimp Skewers as a delicious appetizer or main dish!

Feel free to customize this recipe by adding your favorite herbs or spices to the marinade. You can also grill some vegetables alongside the shrimp for a complete meal.

Baked Chicken Parmesan

Ingredients:

- 4 boneless, skinless chicken breasts
- Salt and pepper to taste
- 1 cup all-purpose flour
- 2 large eggs
- 1 cup breadcrumbs (you can use Italian seasoned breadcrumbs for extra flavor)
- 1 cup grated Parmesan cheese
- 2 cups marinara sauce
- 1 cup shredded mozzarella cheese
- Fresh basil leaves for garnish (optional)
- Cooked spaghetti or your favorite pasta for serving (optional)

Instructions:

1. Preheat your oven to 400°F (200°C). Lightly grease a baking dish with cooking spray or olive oil.
2. Season the chicken breasts with salt and pepper on both sides.
3. Set up a breading station with three shallow dishes: one with flour, one with beaten eggs, and one with a mixture of breadcrumbs and grated Parmesan cheese.
4. Dredge each chicken breast in the flour, shaking off any excess. Dip the floured chicken breast into the beaten eggs, then coat it evenly with the breadcrumb and Parmesan mixture. Press gently to adhere the breadcrumbs to the chicken.
5. Place the breaded chicken breasts in the prepared baking dish. Bake in the preheated oven for 20-25 minutes, or until the chicken is cooked through and the breadcrumbs are golden brown and crispy.
6. Remove the baking dish from the oven and spoon marinara sauce over each chicken breast. Sprinkle shredded mozzarella cheese over the sauce.
7. Return the baking dish to the oven and bake for an additional 5-10 minutes, or until the cheese is melted and bubbly.
8. Once the cheese is melted and bubbly, remove the baking dish from the oven and let it cool for a few minutes before serving.
9. Garnish the Baked Chicken Parmesan with fresh basil leaves, if desired. Serve hot with cooked spaghetti or your favorite pasta on the side.

10. Enjoy your delicious and comforting Baked Chicken Parmesan!

Roasted Vegetable Salad with Balsamic Vinaigrette

Ingredients:

For the Salad:

- 2 cups cherry tomatoes, halved
- 1 red bell pepper, diced
- 1 yellow bell pepper, diced
- 1 zucchini, sliced
- 1 yellow squash, sliced
- 1 red onion, sliced
- 2 tablespoons olive oil
- Salt and pepper to taste
- 6 cups mixed salad greens (such as spinach, arugula, and lettuce)
- 1/4 cup crumbled feta cheese (optional)
- 1/4 cup toasted pine nuts or walnuts (optional)

For the Balsamic Vinaigrette:

- 1/4 cup balsamic vinegar
- 1/4 cup extra virgin olive oil
- 1 tablespoon Dijon mustard
- 1 teaspoon honey or maple syrup
- Salt and pepper to taste

Instructions:

1. Preheat your oven to 400°F (200°C).
2. In a large mixing bowl, combine the cherry tomatoes, diced red and yellow bell peppers, sliced zucchini, sliced yellow squash, and sliced red onion.
3. Drizzle the vegetables with olive oil and season with salt and pepper. Toss until the vegetables are evenly coated with the oil and seasoning.
4. Spread the seasoned vegetables in a single layer on a large baking sheet.

5. Roast the vegetables in the preheated oven for 20-25 minutes, or until they are tender and slightly caramelized, stirring halfway through the cooking time.
6. While the vegetables are roasting, prepare the balsamic vinaigrette. In a small bowl, whisk together the balsamic vinegar, extra virgin olive oil, Dijon mustard, honey or maple syrup, salt, and pepper until well combined.
7. Once the vegetables are roasted, remove them from the oven and let them cool slightly.
8. In a large salad bowl, combine the mixed salad greens with the roasted vegetables.
9. Drizzle the balsamic vinaigrette over the salad and toss gently to coat the vegetables and greens evenly with the dressing.
10. If desired, sprinkle crumbled feta cheese and toasted pine nuts or walnuts over the salad for added flavor and texture.
11. Serve the Roasted Vegetable Salad with Balsamic Vinaigrette immediately as a side dish or light meal.
12. Enjoy your delicious and nutritious Roasted Vegetable Salad with Balsamic Vinaigrette!

Turkey Meatball Soup with Vegetables

Ingredients:

For the Turkey Meatballs:

- 500g ground turkey
- 1/4 cup breadcrumbs
- 1/4 cup grated Parmesan cheese
- 1 egg
- 2 cloves garlic, minced
- 1 teaspoon dried oregano
- 1 teaspoon dried basil
- Salt and pepper to taste

For the Soup:

- 1 tablespoon olive oil
- 1 onion, diced
- 2 carrots, diced
- 2 celery stalks, diced
- 2 cloves garlic, minced
- 6 cups chicken or vegetable broth
- 1 can (400g) diced tomatoes
- 1 cup chopped spinach or kale
- Salt and pepper to taste
- Fresh parsley for garnish (optional)

Instructions:

1. To make the turkey meatballs, in a large mixing bowl, combine ground turkey, breadcrumbs, grated Parmesan cheese, egg, minced garlic, dried oregano, dried basil, salt, and pepper. Mix until well combined.
2. Shape the turkey mixture into small meatballs, about 1-inch in diameter.

3. In a large pot or Dutch oven, heat olive oil over medium heat. Add diced onion, carrots, and celery. Cook for 5-6 minutes until the vegetables start to soften.
4. Add minced garlic to the pot and cook for another minute until fragrant.
5. Pour in the chicken or vegetable broth and diced tomatoes. Bring the soup to a simmer.
6. Gently add the turkey meatballs to the simmering soup. Let the soup simmer for 10-12 minutes, or until the meatballs are cooked through.
7. Stir in chopped spinach or kale and let it cook for another 2-3 minutes until wilted.
8. Season the soup with salt and pepper to taste.
9. Ladle the Turkey Meatball Soup with Vegetables into bowls. Garnish with fresh parsley, if desired.
10. Serve hot and enjoy the comforting and flavorful soup!

Feel free to customize this soup by adding other vegetables such as diced zucchini or bell peppers. You can also add cooked pasta or grains like rice or quinoa for a heartier meal.

Grilled Salmon with Dill and Lemon

Ingredients:

- 4 salmon fillets (about 6 ounces each), skin-on or skinless
- Salt and pepper to taste
- 2 tablespoons olive oil
- 2 tablespoons fresh lemon juice
- 2 cloves garlic, minced
- 1 tablespoon fresh dill, chopped
- Lemon slices for garnish
- Fresh dill sprigs for garnish

Instructions:

1. Preheat your grill to medium-high heat.
2. Season both sides of the salmon fillets with salt and pepper to taste.
3. In a small bowl, whisk together olive oil, lemon juice, minced garlic, and chopped fresh dill.
4. Brush the marinade mixture over the salmon fillets, making sure to coat them evenly.
5. Place the salmon fillets on the preheated grill, skin-side down if they have skin. Close the grill lid and cook for about 4-5 minutes.
6. Carefully flip the salmon fillets using a spatula. Close the grill lid again and cook for an additional 4-5 minutes, or until the salmon is cooked through and flakes easily with a fork.
7. Remove the grilled salmon from the grill and transfer them to a serving platter.
8. Garnish the Grilled Salmon with Dill and Lemon with lemon slices and fresh dill sprigs.
9. Serve hot and enjoy the delicious and flavorful grilled salmon!

You can serve this Grilled Salmon with Dill and Lemon with your favorite side dishes, such as grilled vegetables, rice, or a fresh salad. It's perfect for a light and healthy summer meal!

Spaghetti Squash Primavera

Ingredients:

- 1 medium spaghetti squash
- 2 tablespoons olive oil
- 1 onion, diced
- 2 cloves garlic, minced
- 1 red bell pepper, diced
- 1 yellow bell pepper, diced
- 1 zucchini, diced
- 1 cup cherry tomatoes, halved
- 1/2 cup vegetable broth
- 1/4 cup grated Parmesan cheese (optional)
- Salt and pepper to taste
- Fresh basil or parsley for garnish

Instructions:

1. Preheat your oven to 400°F (200°C). Line a baking sheet with parchment paper.
2. Cut the spaghetti squash in half lengthwise and scoop out the seeds with a spoon. Place the squash halves cut side down on the prepared baking sheet.
3. Bake the spaghetti squash in the preheated oven for 40-45 minutes, or until the flesh is tender and easily pierced with a fork. Remove from the oven and let cool slightly.
4. While the spaghetti squash is baking, heat olive oil in a large skillet over medium heat. Add diced onion and cook until softened, about 3-4 minutes.
5. Add minced garlic to the skillet and cook for another minute until fragrant.
6. Add diced red and yellow bell peppers, diced zucchini, and cherry tomatoes to the skillet. Cook for 5-6 minutes until the vegetables are tender-crisp.
7. Using a fork, scrape the flesh of the cooked spaghetti squash to form "noodles" and add them to the skillet with the cooked vegetables.
8. Pour vegetable broth over the squash and vegetables in the skillet. Stir well to combine.
9. Cook the spaghetti squash primavera mixture for another 2-3 minutes until heated through and the flavors are well combined.

10. Season with salt and pepper to taste. If desired, sprinkle grated Parmesan cheese over the top and stir until melted and incorporated.
11. Garnish the Spaghetti Squash Primavera with fresh basil or parsley before serving.
12. Serve hot and enjoy your delicious and healthy Spaghetti Squash Primavera as a light and flavorful meal!

Feel free to customize this recipe by adding other vegetables or your favorite herbs and spices. It's a versatile dish that's perfect for a nutritious and satisfying dinner!

Quinoa Salad with Chickpeas and Cucumber

Ingredients:

For the Salad:

- 1 cup quinoa, rinsed
- 2 cups water or vegetable broth
- 1 can (15 ounces) chickpeas (garbanzo beans), drained and rinsed
- 1 cucumber, diced
- 1 bell pepper (any color), diced
- 1/2 red onion, finely chopped
- 1/4 cup chopped fresh parsley or cilantro
- Salt and pepper to taste

For the Dressing:

- 1/4 cup extra virgin olive oil
- 2 tablespoons fresh lemon juice
- 1 tablespoon red wine vinegar
- 1 teaspoon Dijon mustard
- 1 clove garlic, minced
- 1/2 teaspoon dried oregano
- Salt and pepper to taste

Instructions:

1. In a medium saucepan, combine quinoa and water or vegetable broth. Bring to a boil, then reduce the heat to low. Cover and simmer for 15-20 minutes, or until the quinoa is cooked and the liquid is absorbed. Remove from heat and let it cool slightly.
2. In a large mixing bowl, combine cooked quinoa, drained and rinsed chickpeas, diced cucumber, diced bell pepper, chopped red onion, and chopped fresh parsley or cilantro. Toss gently to combine.

3. In a small bowl, whisk together extra virgin olive oil, fresh lemon juice, red wine vinegar, Dijon mustard, minced garlic, dried oregano, salt, and pepper to make the dressing.
4. Pour the dressing over the quinoa salad and toss until everything is evenly coated in the dressing.
5. Taste the salad and adjust seasoning with salt and pepper if needed.
6. Cover the bowl and refrigerate the quinoa salad for at least 30 minutes to allow the flavors to meld together.
7. Before serving, give the quinoa salad a final toss and adjust the seasoning if necessary.
8. Serve the Quinoa Salad with Chickpeas and Cucumber chilled or at room temperature as a light and refreshing side dish or a satisfying main course.
9. Enjoy your delicious and nutritious Quinoa Salad with Chickpeas and Cucumber!

Feel free to customize this salad by adding other vegetables, such as cherry tomatoes, shredded carrots, or diced avocado. You can also add crumbled feta cheese or toasted nuts for extra flavor and texture.

Turkey Taco Lettuce Wraps

Ingredients:

For the Turkey Taco Filling:

- 1 tablespoon olive oil
- 1 onion, diced
- 2 cloves garlic, minced
- 500g ground turkey
- 1 packet (about 1 ounce) taco seasoning mix
- 1 can (400g) black beans, drained and rinsed
- 1 cup corn kernels (fresh or frozen)
- 1 cup diced tomatoes (fresh or canned)
- Salt and pepper to taste
- Chopped fresh cilantro for garnish (optional)

For Serving:

- Large lettuce leaves (such as iceberg or romaine)
- Diced avocado
- Sliced cherry tomatoes
- Shredded cheese
- Sour cream or Greek yogurt
- Salsa

Instructions:

1. Heat olive oil in a large skillet over medium heat. Add diced onion and cook until softened, about 3-4 minutes.
2. Add minced garlic to the skillet and cook for another minute until fragrant.
3. Add ground turkey to the skillet and cook, breaking it up with a spoon, until it is browned and cooked through.

4. Stir in taco seasoning mix, black beans, corn kernels, and diced tomatoes. Cook for 5-6 minutes, stirring occasionally, until heated through and the flavors are well combined.
5. Season the turkey taco filling with salt and pepper to taste. Remove from heat and garnish with chopped fresh cilantro, if desired.
6. To serve, spoon the turkey taco filling onto large lettuce leaves, using them as wraps.
7. Top the lettuce wraps with diced avocado, sliced cherry tomatoes, shredded cheese, sour cream or Greek yogurt, and salsa, as desired.
8. Roll up the lettuce leaves around the filling and enjoy your delicious and healthy Turkey Taco Lettuce Wraps!

These Turkey Taco Lettuce Wraps are perfect for a quick and flavorful meal. They're also great for meal prep or as a light lunch or dinner option. Feel free to customize the toppings according to your preferences!

Veggie-packed Minestrone Soup

Ingredients:

- 2 tablespoons olive oil
- 1 onion, diced
- 2 carrots, diced
- 2 celery stalks, diced
- 3 cloves garlic, minced
- 1 zucchini, diced
- 1 yellow squash, diced
- 1 bell pepper (any color), diced
- 1 can (15 ounces) diced tomatoes
- 1 can (15 ounces) kidney beans, drained and rinsed
- 1 can (15 ounces) cannellini beans, drained and rinsed
- 6 cups vegetable broth
- 2 teaspoons dried Italian seasoning
- 1 teaspoon dried oregano
- 1 teaspoon dried basil
- Salt and pepper to taste
- 2 cups chopped spinach or kale
- 1 cup small pasta (such as ditalini or elbow macaroni)
- Grated Parmesan cheese for serving (optional)
- Chopped fresh parsley for garnish (optional)

Instructions:

1. Heat olive oil in a large pot or Dutch oven over medium heat.
2. Add diced onion, carrots, and celery to the pot. Cook for 5-6 minutes until the vegetables start to soften.
3. Add minced garlic to the pot and cook for another minute until fragrant.
4. Stir in diced zucchini, yellow squash, and bell pepper. Cook for 5 minutes until the vegetables are tender-crisp.
5. Add diced tomatoes (with their juices), kidney beans, cannellini beans, vegetable broth, dried Italian seasoning, dried oregano, and dried basil to the pot. Season with salt and pepper to taste.

6. Bring the soup to a simmer, then reduce the heat to low. Cover and let it simmer for 20-25 minutes, stirring occasionally.
7. Stir in chopped spinach or kale and small pasta. Cook for another 8-10 minutes, or until the pasta is al dente and the greens are wilted.
8. Taste the soup and adjust the seasoning if needed.
9. Ladle the Veggie-packed Minestrone Soup into bowls. Serve hot, garnished with grated Parmesan cheese and chopped fresh parsley, if desired.
10. Enjoy your hearty and nutritious Veggie-packed Minestrone Soup as a comforting meal!

This soup is packed with vegetables and fiber-rich beans, making it both delicious and satisfying. Feel free to customize the recipe by adding your favorite vegetables or herbs.

Lemon Herb Tilapia

Ingredients:

- 4 tilapia fillets
- Salt and pepper to taste
- 2 tablespoons olive oil
- 2 cloves garlic, minced
- Zest of 1 lemon
- Juice of 1 lemon
- 1 teaspoon dried thyme
- 1 teaspoon dried oregano
- 1 teaspoon dried parsley
- Lemon slices for garnish
- Fresh parsley for garnish

Instructions:

1. Preheat your oven to 375°F (190°C).
2. Season both sides of the tilapia fillets with salt and pepper.
3. In a small bowl, whisk together olive oil, minced garlic, lemon zest, lemon juice, dried thyme, dried oregano, and dried parsley.
4. Place the tilapia fillets in a baking dish that has been lightly greased with olive oil or cooking spray.
5. Pour the lemon herb mixture over the tilapia fillets, making sure to coat them evenly.
6. Arrange lemon slices on top of the tilapia fillets.
7. Bake the tilapia in the preheated oven for 12-15 minutes, or until the fish is cooked through and flakes easily with a fork.
8. Once the tilapia is cooked, remove it from the oven and garnish with fresh parsley.
9. Serve the Lemon Herb Tilapia hot, accompanied by your favorite side dishes such as steamed vegetables, rice, or salad.
10. Enjoy your delicious and aromatic Lemon Herb Tilapia!

This dish is quick and easy to prepare, making it perfect for a weeknight dinner. The combination of lemon and herbs adds a bright and flavorful touch to the mild-tasting tilapia.

Ratatouille

Ingredients:

- 1 large eggplant, diced
- 2 zucchini, diced
- 1 yellow bell pepper, diced
- 1 red bell pepper, diced
- 1 onion, diced
- 3 cloves garlic, minced
- 4 tomatoes, diced
- 2 tablespoons tomato paste
- 2 tablespoons olive oil
- 1 teaspoon dried thyme
- 1 teaspoon dried oregano
- Salt and pepper to taste
- Fresh basil or parsley for garnish (optional)

Instructions:

1. Heat olive oil in a large skillet or Dutch oven over medium heat.
2. Add diced onion to the skillet and cook for 3-4 minutes until softened.
3. Add minced garlic to the skillet and cook for another minute until fragrant.
4. Add diced eggplant, zucchini, yellow bell pepper, and red bell pepper to the skillet. Cook for 5-6 minutes until the vegetables start to soften.
5. Stir in diced tomatoes, tomato paste, dried thyme, dried oregano, salt, and pepper. Mix well to combine.
6. Cover the skillet and let the ratatouille simmer over medium-low heat for 20-25 minutes, stirring occasionally, until the vegetables are tender and the flavors are well blended.
7. Taste and adjust the seasoning if necessary.
8. Once the ratatouille is cooked, remove it from heat and let it cool slightly.
9. Serve the Ratatouille hot or at room temperature, garnished with fresh basil or parsley if desired.
10. Enjoy your delicious and hearty Ratatouille as a side dish, main course, or served over cooked pasta or rice.

Ratatouille is a versatile dish that can be enjoyed on its own or paired with your favorite protein for a complete meal. It's also great for meal prep and can be stored in the refrigerator for a few days or frozen for longer-term storage.

Turkey and Sweet Potato Hash

Ingredients:

- 2 tablespoons olive oil
- 1 onion, diced
- 2 cloves garlic, minced
- 2 medium sweet potatoes, peeled and diced into small cubes
- 1 red bell pepper, diced
- 1 green bell pepper, diced
- 500g ground turkey
- 1 teaspoon smoked paprika
- 1 teaspoon dried thyme
- Salt and pepper to taste
- Fresh parsley for garnish (optional)
- Fried or poached eggs for serving (optional)

Instructions:

1. Heat olive oil in a large skillet or frying pan over medium heat.
2. Add diced onion to the skillet and cook for 3-4 minutes until softened.
3. Add minced garlic to the skillet and cook for another minute until fragrant.
4. Add diced sweet potatoes to the skillet and cook for 8-10 minutes, stirring occasionally, until they start to soften and brown slightly.
5. Stir in diced red bell pepper and green bell pepper, and cook for another 5 minutes until the peppers are tender-crisp.
6. Push the vegetables to the side of the skillet and add ground turkey to the center. Break up the turkey with a spoon and cook for 5-6 minutes until browned and cooked through.
7. Stir the cooked turkey into the vegetable mixture in the skillet.
8. Season the turkey and sweet potato hash with smoked paprika, dried thyme, salt, and pepper. Mix well to combine.
9. Cook for another 2-3 minutes until the flavors are well blended and the hash is heated through.
10. Taste and adjust the seasoning if necessary.
11. Garnish the Turkey and Sweet Potato Hash with fresh parsley if desired.
12. Serve the hash hot, with fried or poached eggs on top if desired.

13. Enjoy your delicious and hearty Turkey and Sweet Potato Hash for breakfast, brunch, or any time of the day!

This dish is filling, flavorful, and packed with nutritious ingredients. It's perfect for a satisfying meal that's quick and easy to make.

Grilled Vegetable Skewers

Ingredients:

- Assorted vegetables, such as cherry tomatoes, bell peppers, zucchini, yellow squash, red onion, mushrooms, and eggplant
- Olive oil
- Salt and pepper
- Optional seasonings: garlic powder, onion powder, paprika, dried herbs (such as thyme or rosemary)
- Wooden or metal skewers

Instructions:

1. If you're using wooden skewers, soak them in water for at least 30 minutes to prevent them from burning on the grill.
2. Prepare the vegetables by washing and cutting them into bite-sized pieces. Try to cut them into similar-sized pieces so they cook evenly.
3. Preheat your grill to medium-high heat.
4. Thread the vegetables onto the skewers, alternating different types of vegetables for a colorful presentation.
5. Brush the skewered vegetables with olive oil and season with salt, pepper, and any other desired seasonings.
6. Place the vegetable skewers on the preheated grill. Cook for 8-10 minutes, turning occasionally, until the vegetables are tender and lightly charred.
7. Remove the skewers from the grill and transfer them to a serving platter.
8. Serve the grilled vegetable skewers hot as a side dish or as a main course. They're delicious on their own or served with a dipping sauce or drizzle of balsamic glaze.
9. Enjoy your flavorful and nutritious grilled vegetable skewers!

Feel free to customize this recipe by using your favorite vegetables or adding tofu or marinated tempeh for protein. You can also brush the skewers with a marinade or barbecue sauce for extra flavor.

Lentil Soup with Spinach and Tomatoes

Ingredients:

- 1 cup dried green or brown lentils, rinsed and drained
- 1 tablespoon olive oil
- 1 onion, diced
- 2 carrots, diced
- 2 celery stalks, diced
- 3 cloves garlic, minced
- 1 teaspoon ground cumin
- 1 teaspoon ground coriander
- 1/2 teaspoon smoked paprika
- 1 can (400g) diced tomatoes
- 4 cups vegetable broth
- 2 cups fresh spinach leaves, chopped
- Salt and pepper to taste
- Fresh parsley for garnish (optional)
- Lemon wedges for serving (optional)

Instructions:

1. Heat olive oil in a large pot or Dutch oven over medium heat.
2. Add diced onion, carrots, and celery to the pot. Cook for 5-6 minutes until the vegetables start to soften.
3. Add minced garlic to the pot and cook for another minute until fragrant.
4. Stir in ground cumin, ground coriander, and smoked paprika. Cook for another minute until the spices are fragrant.
5. Add rinsed and drained lentils, diced tomatoes (with their juices), and vegetable broth to the pot. Stir to combine.
6. Bring the soup to a simmer, then reduce the heat to low. Cover and let it simmer for 20-25 minutes, or until the lentils are tender.
7. Stir in chopped fresh spinach leaves and let them wilt in the hot soup for a few minutes.
8. Taste the soup and season with salt and pepper to taste.
9. Ladle the Lentil Soup with Spinach and Tomatoes into bowls. Garnish with fresh parsley if desired.

10. Serve hot, with lemon wedges on the side for squeezing over the soup if desired.
11. Enjoy your hearty and flavorful Lentil Soup with Spinach and Tomatoes!

This soup is packed with protein-rich lentils, nutritious vegetables, and aromatic spices. It's perfect for a cozy meal on a chilly day and leftovers can be stored in the refrigerator for a few days or frozen for longer-term storage.

Baked Chicken Tenders with Honey Mustard Sauce

Ingredients:

For the Chicken Tenders:

- 500g chicken breast tenders
- 1 cup breadcrumbs (panko or regular)
- 1/4 cup grated Parmesan cheese
- 1 teaspoon garlic powder
- 1 teaspoon paprika
- Salt and pepper to taste
- 2 eggs, beaten

For the Honey Mustard Sauce:

- 1/4 cup mayonnaise
- 2 tablespoons Dijon mustard
- 2 tablespoons honey
- 1 tablespoon lemon juice
- Salt and pepper to taste

Instructions:

1. Preheat your oven to 400°F (200°C). Line a baking sheet with parchment paper or lightly grease it with cooking spray.
2. In a shallow dish, combine breadcrumbs, grated Parmesan cheese, garlic powder, paprika, salt, and pepper. Mix well to combine.
3. Dip each chicken tender into the beaten eggs, then coat it evenly with the breadcrumb mixture. Press gently to adhere the breadcrumbs to the chicken.
4. Place the coated chicken tenders on the prepared baking sheet in a single layer.
5. Bake in the preheated oven for 15-20 minutes, or until the chicken tenders are golden brown and cooked through, flipping halfway through cooking.
6. While the chicken tenders are baking, prepare the honey mustard sauce. In a small bowl, whisk together mayonnaise, Dijon mustard, honey, lemon juice, salt, and pepper until smooth and well combined.

7. Once the chicken tenders are cooked, remove them from the oven and let them cool slightly.
8. Serve the Baked Chicken Tenders hot with the Honey Mustard Sauce on the side for dipping.
9. Enjoy your crispy and flavorful Baked Chicken Tenders with Honey Mustard Sauce as a delicious appetizer or main dish!

These chicken tenders are healthier than their fried counterparts, but still crispy and full of flavor. The honey mustard sauce adds a sweet and tangy kick that pairs perfectly with the juicy chicken.

Tofu Stir-Fry with Broccoli and Bell Peppers

Ingredients:

For the Stir-Fry Sauce:

- 1/4 cup soy sauce (or tamari for gluten-free)
- 2 tablespoons rice vinegar
- 2 tablespoons hoisin sauce
- 1 tablespoon honey or maple syrup
- 1 teaspoon sesame oil
- 1 teaspoon cornstarch
- 1/4 cup water

For the Stir-Fry:

- 350g firm tofu, pressed and cubed
- 2 tablespoons cornstarch
- 2 tablespoons vegetable oil
- 2 cups broccoli florets
- 1 red bell pepper, sliced
- 1 yellow bell pepper, sliced
- 3 cloves garlic, minced
- 1 tablespoon grated ginger
- Cooked rice or noodles for serving
- Sesame seeds and chopped green onions for garnish (optional)

Instructions:

1. In a small bowl, whisk together all the ingredients for the stir-fry sauce: soy sauce, rice vinegar, hoisin sauce, honey or maple syrup, sesame oil, cornstarch, and water. Set aside.
2. Press the tofu to remove excess water: Wrap the tofu block in paper towels and place it between two plates. Place a heavy object on top (such as a cast-iron skillet or canned goods) and let it press for about 20-30 minutes. Then, cut the

pressed tofu into cubes and toss them with 2 tablespoons of cornstarch until evenly coated.
3. Heat 1 tablespoon of vegetable oil in a large skillet or wok over medium-high heat. Add the tofu cubes and cook until golden brown and crispy on all sides, about 5-7 minutes. Remove the tofu from the skillet and set aside.
4. In the same skillet, add another tablespoon of vegetable oil. Add the broccoli florets and sliced bell peppers. Stir-fry for about 4-5 minutes, until the vegetables are tender-crisp.
5. Add the minced garlic and grated ginger to the skillet. Stir-fry for another minute until fragrant.
6. Return the cooked tofu to the skillet with the vegetables.
7. Pour the prepared stir-fry sauce over the tofu and vegetables in the skillet. Stir well to coat everything evenly in the sauce.
8. Cook for another 2-3 minutes, until the sauce has thickened and everything is heated through.
9. Serve the Tofu Stir-Fry with Broccoli and Bell Peppers hot over cooked rice or noodles.
10. Garnish with sesame seeds and chopped green onions, if desired.
11. Enjoy your delicious and flavorful Tofu Stir-Fry with Broccoli and Bell Peppers!

This stir-fry is packed with protein from the tofu and plenty of veggies, making it a nutritious and satisfying meal. Feel free to customize the recipe by adding other vegetables or adjusting the seasonings to your taste.

Cauliflower Fried Rice

Ingredients:

- 1 medium head of cauliflower
- 2 tablespoons vegetable oil or sesame oil
- 2 cloves garlic, minced
- 1 small onion, diced
- 1 carrot, diced
- 1/2 cup frozen peas
- 2 eggs, beaten
- 3 tablespoons soy sauce (or tamari for gluten-free)
- 1 tablespoon oyster sauce (optional)
- Salt and pepper to taste
- Green onions, chopped, for garnish (optional)
- Sesame seeds, for garnish (optional)

Instructions:

1. Cut the cauliflower into florets and discard the core. Place the florets in a food processor and pulse until they resemble rice or couscous.
2. Heat 1 tablespoon of oil in a large skillet or wok over medium-high heat. Add the minced garlic and diced onion, and cook for 2-3 minutes until softened and fragrant.
3. Add the diced carrot and cook for another 2-3 minutes until slightly softened.
4. Push the vegetables to the side of the skillet and add the beaten eggs to the empty space. Scramble the eggs until cooked through, then mix them with the vegetables.
5. Push the vegetable and egg mixture to the side of the skillet again, and add the remaining tablespoon of oil to the empty space. Add the riced cauliflower and cook for 4-5 minutes, stirring occasionally, until it starts to soften.
6. Add the frozen peas to the skillet and cook for another 2-3 minutes until heated through.
7. Stir in the soy sauce and oyster sauce (if using), and season with salt and pepper to taste. Mix well to combine all the ingredients.
8. Cook for another 2-3 minutes, stirring occasionally, until everything is heated through and well combined.

9. Remove the skillet from heat and garnish the Cauliflower Fried Rice with chopped green onions and sesame seeds, if desired.
10. Serve hot as a main dish or side dish.
11. Enjoy your tasty and nutritious Cauliflower Fried Rice!

This Cauliflower Fried Rice is a great way to enjoy a classic dish with fewer carbs and more veggies. It's versatile, customizable, and packed with flavor!

Lemon Herb Grilled Chicken

Ingredients:

- 4 boneless, skinless chicken breasts
- Zest of 1 lemon
- Juice of 2 lemons
- 3 cloves garlic, minced
- 2 tablespoons fresh herbs (such as parsley, thyme, rosemary, or oregano), chopped
- 2 tablespoons olive oil
- Salt and pepper to taste

Instructions:

1. In a small bowl, whisk together the lemon zest, lemon juice, minced garlic, chopped fresh herbs, olive oil, salt, and pepper to make the marinade.
2. Place the chicken breasts in a shallow dish or resealable plastic bag. Pour the marinade over the chicken, making sure it's well coated. Marinate the chicken in the refrigerator for at least 30 minutes, or up to 4 hours, turning occasionally.
3. Preheat your grill to medium-high heat. Make sure the grill grates are clean and lightly oiled to prevent sticking.
4. Remove the chicken from the marinade, shaking off any excess marinade, and discard the remaining marinade.
5. Place the chicken breasts on the preheated grill. Grill for 6-8 minutes per side, or until the chicken is cooked through and no longer pink in the center. The internal temperature should reach 165°F (75°C).
6. Once the chicken is cooked, remove it from the grill and let it rest for a few minutes before serving.
7. Serve the Lemon Herb Grilled Chicken hot, garnished with additional chopped fresh herbs and lemon slices if desired.
8. Enjoy your delicious and aromatic Lemon Herb Grilled Chicken!

This chicken is perfect for a summer barbecue or any time you want a quick and flavorful meal. It pairs well with a variety of sides, such as grilled vegetables, salad, or rice.

Greek Salad with Grilled Chicken

Ingredients:

For the Grilled Chicken:

- 4 boneless, skinless chicken breasts
- 2 tablespoons olive oil
- 2 cloves garlic, minced
- 1 teaspoon dried oregano
- 1 teaspoon dried thyme
- Salt and pepper to taste

For the Greek Salad:

- 1 large cucumber, diced
- 4 medium tomatoes, diced
- 1 red onion, thinly sliced
- 1 green bell pepper, diced
- 1/2 cup Kalamata olives, pitted
- 1/2 cup crumbled feta cheese
- Fresh parsley or oregano for garnish (optional)

For the Greek Salad Dressing:

- 1/4 cup extra virgin olive oil
- 2 tablespoons red wine vinegar
- 1 teaspoon dried oregano
- Salt and pepper to taste

Instructions:

1. In a small bowl, whisk together the ingredients for the Greek Salad Dressing: olive oil, red wine vinegar, dried oregano, salt, and pepper. Set aside.

2. In a separate bowl, prepare the marinade for the grilled chicken: mix together olive oil, minced garlic, dried oregano, dried thyme, salt, and pepper.
3. Place the chicken breasts in a shallow dish or resealable plastic bag. Pour the marinade over the chicken, making sure it's well coated. Marinate the chicken in the refrigerator for at least 30 minutes, or up to 4 hours.
4. Preheat your grill to medium-high heat. Make sure the grill grates are clean and lightly oiled to prevent sticking.
5. Remove the chicken from the marinade and discard any excess marinade. Grill the chicken breasts for 6-8 minutes per side, or until they are cooked through and no longer pink in the center. The internal temperature should reach 165°F (75°C). Once cooked, remove the chicken from the grill and let it rest for a few minutes before slicing.
6. While the chicken is resting, prepare the Greek salad. In a large bowl, combine diced cucumber, diced tomatoes, sliced red onion, diced green bell pepper, and Kalamata olives.
7. Pour the Greek Salad Dressing over the salad and toss gently to coat all the ingredients.
8. To serve, divide the Greek salad among serving plates. Top each plate with sliced grilled chicken breasts.
9. Sprinkle crumbled feta cheese over the salads and garnish with fresh parsley or oregano if desired.
10. Enjoy your delicious and flavorful Greek Salad with Grilled Chicken!

This salad is fresh, vibrant, and packed with Mediterranean flavors. It's perfect for a light and healthy meal, whether you're dining al fresco or looking for a quick weeknight dinner option.

Baked Eggplant Parmesan

Ingredients:

- 2 large eggplants, sliced into 1/2-inch rounds
- Salt
- 2 cups Italian-style breadcrumbs (or panko breadcrumbs)
- 1 cup grated Parmesan cheese
- 2 eggs, beaten
- 2 cups marinara sauce
- 2 cups shredded mozzarella cheese
- Fresh basil leaves for garnish (optional)
- Olive oil, for drizzling

Instructions:

1. Preheat your oven to 400°F (200°C). Line two baking sheets with parchment paper or lightly grease them with olive oil.
2. Place the eggplant slices in a colander and sprinkle them with salt. Let them sit for about 30 minutes to release excess moisture. Pat the eggplant slices dry with paper towels.
3. In a shallow dish, combine the Italian-style breadcrumbs with grated Parmesan cheese. Mix well.
4. Dip each eggplant slice into the beaten eggs, then coat it evenly with the breadcrumb mixture. Press gently to adhere the breadcrumbs to the eggplant.
5. Place the breaded eggplant slices on the prepared baking sheets in a single layer. Drizzle lightly with olive oil.
6. Bake the eggplant slices in the preheated oven for 20-25 minutes, flipping them halfway through baking, until they are golden brown and crispy.
7. Remove the baked eggplant slices from the oven and reduce the oven temperature to 350°F (175°C).
8. In a baking dish, spread a thin layer of marinara sauce on the bottom. Place a layer of baked eggplant slices on top of the sauce, overlapping slightly if necessary.
9. Spoon more marinara sauce over the eggplant slices, then sprinkle shredded mozzarella cheese on top.

10. Repeat the layers until all the eggplant slices, marinara sauce, and mozzarella cheese are used, finishing with a layer of cheese on top.
11. Cover the baking dish with aluminum foil and bake in the preheated oven for 25-30 minutes, until the cheese is melted and bubbly.
12. Remove the foil and bake for an additional 5-10 minutes, or until the cheese is golden brown and bubbly.
13. Remove the baked eggplant Parmesan from the oven and let it cool for a few minutes before serving.
14. Garnish with fresh basil leaves if desired.
15. Serve the Baked Eggplant Parmesan hot as a delicious and satisfying meal!

This dish is a healthier twist on the classic Eggplant Parmesan, with the eggplant slices baked instead of fried. It's cheesy, comforting, and perfect for a cozy dinner at home. Enjoy!

Shrimp and Vegetable Stir-Fry with Brown Rice

Ingredients:

For the Stir-Fry:

- 500g shrimp, peeled and deveined
- 2 tablespoons soy sauce (or tamari for gluten-free)
- 2 tablespoons oyster sauce
- 1 tablespoon sesame oil
- 2 cloves garlic, minced
- 1 teaspoon grated ginger
- 1 tablespoon vegetable oil
- 1 onion, thinly sliced
- 2 bell peppers (any color), thinly sliced
- 2 cups broccoli florets
- 1 cup snap peas, trimmed
- Salt and pepper to taste
- Sesame seeds for garnish (optional)
- Sliced green onions for garnish (optional)

For the Brown Rice:

- 1 cup brown rice
- 2 cups water
- Pinch of salt

Instructions:

1. Start by cooking the brown rice. In a medium saucepan, combine the brown rice, water, and a pinch of salt. Bring to a boil over high heat, then reduce the heat to low, cover, and simmer for 40-45 minutes, or until the rice is tender and all the water is absorbed. Fluff the rice with a fork and set aside.
2. In a small bowl, mix together the soy sauce, oyster sauce, and sesame oil to make the sauce for the stir-fry. Set aside.

3. Heat the vegetable oil in a large skillet or wok over medium-high heat. Add the minced garlic and grated ginger, and cook for 1 minute until fragrant.
4. Add the sliced onion to the skillet and cook for 2-3 minutes until softened.
5. Add the bell peppers, broccoli florets, and snap peas to the skillet. Stir-fry for 4-5 minutes until the vegetables are crisp-tender.
6. Push the vegetables to the side of the skillet and add the shrimp to the empty space. Cook the shrimp for 2-3 minutes per side until pink and cooked through.
7. Stir the shrimp into the vegetables in the skillet.
8. Pour the sauce over the shrimp and vegetables in the skillet. Stir well to coat everything evenly in the sauce.
9. Cook for another 1-2 minutes, until the sauce is heated through and slightly thickened.
10. Taste and adjust the seasoning with salt and pepper if needed.
11. Remove the skillet from heat and serve the Shrimp and Vegetable Stir-Fry hot over cooked brown rice.
12. Garnish with sesame seeds and sliced green onions if desired.
13. Enjoy your delicious and nutritious Shrimp and Vegetable Stir-Fry with Brown Rice!

This dish is quick and easy to make, packed with protein and veggies, and bursting with flavor. It's perfect for a healthy weeknight dinner that the whole family will love!

Turkey and Black Bean Chili

Ingredients:

- 1 tablespoon olive oil
- 1 onion, diced
- 3 cloves garlic, minced
- 500g ground turkey
- 1 can (400g) black beans, drained and rinsed
- 1 can (400g) diced tomatoes
- 1 red bell pepper, diced
- 1 green bell pepper, diced
- 2 tablespoons tomato paste
- 2 teaspoons chili powder
- 1 teaspoon ground cumin
- 1 teaspoon paprika
- 1/2 teaspoon dried oregano
- Salt and pepper to taste
- 2 cups chicken or vegetable broth
- Optional toppings: shredded cheddar cheese, sour cream, sliced green onions, chopped cilantro, diced avocado

Instructions:

1. Heat olive oil in a large pot or Dutch oven over medium heat.
2. Add diced onion and minced garlic to the pot. Cook for 3-4 minutes until softened and fragrant.
3. Add ground turkey to the pot. Cook, breaking up the turkey with a spoon, until browned and cooked through, about 5-6 minutes.
4. Stir in diced bell peppers, black beans, diced tomatoes, tomato paste, chili powder, ground cumin, paprika, dried oregano, salt, and pepper.
5. Pour in chicken or vegetable broth and stir to combine all the ingredients.
6. Bring the chili to a simmer, then reduce the heat to low. Cover and let it simmer for 20-25 minutes, stirring occasionally, to allow the flavors to meld together and the chili to thicken.
7. Taste and adjust the seasoning with more salt and pepper if needed.
8. Once the chili is cooked and thickened to your liking, remove it from heat.

9. Serve the Turkey and Black Bean Chili hot, garnished with your favorite toppings such as shredded cheddar cheese, sour cream, sliced green onions, chopped cilantro, or diced avocado.
10. Enjoy your delicious and comforting Turkey and Black Bean Chili!

This chili is packed with protein, fiber, and flavor, making it a satisfying and nutritious meal. It's perfect for a cozy dinner on a chilly evening or for meal prep to enjoy throughout the week.

Baked Zucchini Fries

Ingredients:

- 2 medium zucchinis
- 1/2 cup all-purpose flour (or almond flour for a gluten-free option)
- 2 eggs, beaten
- 1 cup breadcrumbs (panko or regular)
- 1/4 cup grated Parmesan cheese
- 1 teaspoon garlic powder
- 1 teaspoon dried Italian seasoning (or dried oregano)
- Salt and pepper to taste
- Cooking spray or olive oil for greasing

Instructions:

1. Preheat your oven to 425°F (220°C). Line a baking sheet with parchment paper or lightly grease it with cooking spray or olive oil.
2. Cut the zucchinis into thin strips, resembling French fries.
3. Set up a breading station with three shallow bowls. Place the flour in the first bowl, beaten eggs in the second bowl, and breadcrumbs mixed with grated Parmesan cheese, garlic powder, dried Italian seasoning, salt, and pepper in the third bowl.
4. Dredge each zucchini strip in the flour, shaking off any excess.
5. Dip the floured zucchini strip into the beaten eggs, allowing any excess to drip off.
6. Coat the zucchini strip with the breadcrumb mixture, pressing gently to adhere the breadcrumbs to the zucchini.
7. Place the coated zucchini strip on the prepared baking sheet. Repeat the process with the remaining zucchini strips.
8. Lightly spray the coated zucchini fries with cooking spray or drizzle them with olive oil.
9. Bake in the preheated oven for 20-25 minutes, flipping halfway through cooking, until the zucchini fries are golden brown and crispy.
10. Once cooked, remove the zucchini fries from the oven and let them cool for a few minutes before serving.

11. Serve the Baked Zucchini Fries hot as a delicious and healthier alternative to traditional fries.
12. Enjoy your crispy and flavorful Baked Zucchini Fries with your favorite dipping sauce, such as marinara sauce, ranch dressing, or aioli!

These zucchini fries are a great way to enjoy the crispiness of fries with the added benefit of being baked instead of fried. They're perfect as a snack, appetizer, or side dish for any occasion.

Asian-style Tofu Lettuce Wraps

Ingredients:

For the Tofu Marinade:

- 400g extra firm tofu, pressed and cubed
- 2 tablespoons soy sauce (or tamari for gluten-free)
- 1 tablespoon hoisin sauce
- 1 tablespoon rice vinegar
- 1 teaspoon sesame oil
- 1 teaspoon grated ginger
- 2 cloves garlic, minced

For the Lettuce Wraps:

- 1 tablespoon vegetable oil
- 1 onion, diced
- 2 bell peppers (any color), diced
- 1 cup mushrooms, diced
- 1 carrot, grated
- 1/2 cup water chestnuts, chopped
- 1/4 cup green onions, sliced
- 1 head iceberg or butter lettuce, leaves separated
- Sesame seeds and sliced green onions for garnish (optional)

For the Sauce:

- 2 tablespoons soy sauce (or tamari for gluten-free)
- 1 tablespoon hoisin sauce
- 1 tablespoon rice vinegar
- 1 teaspoon sesame oil
- 1 teaspoon sriracha (optional, for heat)

Instructions:

1. Start by preparing the tofu marinade. In a bowl, whisk together soy sauce, hoisin sauce, rice vinegar, sesame oil, grated ginger, and minced garlic. Add the cubed tofu and toss to coat. Let it marinate for at least 30 minutes, or up to 2 hours.
2. While the tofu is marinating, prepare the vegetables. Heat vegetable oil in a large skillet or wok over medium-high heat. Add diced onion and cook for 2-3 minutes until softened.
3. Add diced bell peppers and mushrooms to the skillet. Cook for another 3-4 minutes until the vegetables are tender.
4. Stir in grated carrot and water chestnuts. Cook for another 2 minutes, then add sliced green onions. Remove the vegetable mixture from the skillet and set aside.
5. In the same skillet, add the marinated tofu cubes (reserve the marinade). Cook the tofu for 5-6 minutes, stirring occasionally, until browned and slightly crispy on the outside.
6. While the tofu is cooking, prepare the sauce. In a small bowl, whisk together soy sauce, hoisin sauce, rice vinegar, sesame oil, and sriracha (if using).
7. Once the tofu is cooked, return the vegetable mixture to the skillet. Pour the sauce over the tofu and vegetables, along with the reserved marinade. Stir well to coat everything evenly in the sauce.
8. Cook for another 2-3 minutes, until the sauce is heated through and slightly thickened.
9. To serve, spoon the tofu and vegetable mixture into lettuce leaves. Garnish with sesame seeds and sliced green onions if desired.
10. Enjoy your delicious and flavorful Asian-style Tofu Lettuce Wraps!

These lettuce wraps are packed with protein and veggies, making them a nutritious and satisfying meal. They're perfect for a light lunch, dinner, or as a party appetizer. Adjust the amount of sriracha to your desired level of spiciness.

Mediterranean Chickpea Salad

Ingredients:

For the Salad:

- 2 cans (400g each) chickpeas, drained and rinsed
- 1 cucumber, diced
- 1 red bell pepper, diced
- 1 yellow bell pepper, diced
- 1 cup cherry tomatoes, halved
- 1/2 red onion, finely chopped
- 1/2 cup Kalamata olives, pitted and halved
- 1/4 cup chopped fresh parsley
- 1/4 cup chopped fresh mint (optional)

For the Dressing:

- 1/4 cup extra virgin olive oil
- 2 tablespoons red wine vinegar
- 1 clove garlic, minced
- 1 teaspoon dried oregano
- Salt and pepper to taste

Instructions:

1. In a large mixing bowl, combine the chickpeas, diced cucumber, diced bell peppers, halved cherry tomatoes, finely chopped red onion, halved Kalamata olives, chopped fresh parsley, and chopped fresh mint (if using). Mix well to combine.
2. In a small bowl, whisk together the extra virgin olive oil, red wine vinegar, minced garlic, dried oregano, salt, and pepper to make the dressing.
3. Pour the dressing over the chickpea salad and toss until everything is evenly coated in the dressing.
4. Taste and adjust the seasoning with more salt and pepper if needed.

5. Cover the bowl with plastic wrap or transfer the salad to an airtight container. Refrigerate for at least 30 minutes to allow the flavors to meld together.
6. Before serving, give the Mediterranean Chickpea Salad a final toss. Garnish with additional chopped fresh parsley or mint if desired.
7. Serve the salad chilled as a delicious and nutritious side dish or light meal.
8. Enjoy your flavorful and vibrant Mediterranean Chickpea Salad!

This salad is packed with protein, fiber, and vitamins, making it a healthy and satisfying option for lunch or dinner. It's also perfect for picnics, potlucks, or as a side dish for grilled meats or seafood. Feel free to customize the salad by adding other Mediterranean-inspired ingredients such as feta cheese, artichoke hearts, or roasted red peppers.

Lemon Garlic Baked Cod

Ingredients:

- 4 cod fillets (about 6 ounces each)
- 2 tablespoons olive oil
- 2 cloves garlic, minced
- Zest of 1 lemon
- Juice of 1 lemon
- 1 teaspoon dried oregano
- Salt and pepper to taste
- Fresh parsley, chopped, for garnish (optional)
- Lemon slices for serving (optional)

Instructions:

1. Preheat your oven to 400°F (200°C). Line a baking dish with parchment paper or lightly grease it with olive oil.
2. Pat the cod fillets dry with paper towels and place them in the prepared baking dish.
3. In a small bowl, whisk together the olive oil, minced garlic, lemon zest, lemon juice, dried oregano, salt, and pepper.
4. Pour the lemon garlic mixture over the cod fillets, making sure they are evenly coated.
5. Bake the cod fillets in the preheated oven for 12-15 minutes, or until the fish is opaque and flakes easily with a fork.
6. Remove the baked cod from the oven and let it rest for a few minutes.
7. Garnish the cod fillets with chopped fresh parsley and lemon slices if desired.
8. Serve the Lemon Garlic Baked Cod hot, accompanied by your favorite side dishes such as roasted vegetables, rice, or salad.
9. Enjoy your tender and flavorful Lemon Garlic Baked Cod!

This dish is quick and easy to prepare, yet elegant enough for a special dinner. The combination of lemon and garlic adds brightness and depth of flavor to the delicate cod fillets. It's a healthy and delicious meal that's perfect for any occasion.

Turkey and Spinach Stuffed Bell Peppers

Ingredients:

- 4 large bell peppers (any color), halved and seeds removed
- 1 tablespoon olive oil
- 1 onion, diced
- 2 cloves garlic, minced
- 500g ground turkey
- 2 cups fresh spinach, chopped
- 1 can (400g) diced tomatoes, drained
- 1 cup cooked quinoa or rice
- 1 teaspoon dried oregano
- 1 teaspoon dried basil
- Salt and pepper to taste
- 1 cup shredded mozzarella cheese
- Fresh parsley, chopped, for garnish (optional)

Instructions:

1. Preheat your oven to 375°F (190°C). Arrange the halved bell peppers in a baking dish, cut side up.
2. In a large skillet, heat olive oil over medium heat. Add diced onion and minced garlic, and cook until softened and fragrant, about 3-4 minutes.
3. Add ground turkey to the skillet and cook until browned, breaking it up with a spoon as it cooks, about 5-6 minutes.
4. Stir in chopped spinach and cook until wilted, about 2-3 minutes.
5. Add diced tomatoes, cooked quinoa or rice, dried oregano, dried basil, salt, and pepper to the skillet. Stir well to combine all the ingredients.
6. Remove the skillet from heat and taste the filling, adjusting seasoning if needed.
7. Spoon the turkey and spinach mixture evenly into each halved bell pepper, pressing it down gently.
8. Cover the baking dish with aluminum foil and bake in the preheated oven for 25-30 minutes, or until the peppers are tender.
9. Remove the foil from the baking dish and sprinkle shredded mozzarella cheese over each stuffed bell pepper.

10. Return the baking dish to the oven and bake for an additional 5-7 minutes, or until the cheese is melted and bubbly.
11. Remove the stuffed bell peppers from the oven and let them cool for a few minutes before serving.
12. Garnish with chopped fresh parsley if desired.
13. Serve the Turkey and Spinach Stuffed Bell Peppers hot as a delicious and nutritious meal!

These stuffed bell peppers are packed with protein, vegetables, and whole grains, making them a healthy and satisfying option for lunch or dinner. They're also great for meal prep and can be reheated for a quick and easy meal throughout the week. Enjoy!

Baked Falafel with Tzatziki Sauce

Ingredients:

For the Falafel:

- 2 cans (400g each) chickpeas, drained and rinsed
- 1 small onion, chopped
- 3 cloves garlic, minced
- 1/4 cup fresh parsley, chopped
- 1/4 cup fresh cilantro, chopped
- 2 tablespoons olive oil
- 2 tablespoons lemon juice
- 2 teaspoons ground cumin
- 1 teaspoon ground coriander
- 1 teaspoon baking powder
- Salt and pepper to taste
- 1/4 cup breadcrumbs (optional, for binding)

For the Tzatziki Sauce:

- 1 cup Greek yogurt
- 1/2 cucumber, grated and squeezed to remove excess moisture
- 1 clove garlic, minced
- 1 tablespoon fresh lemon juice
- 1 tablespoon fresh dill, chopped (or 1 teaspoon dried dill)
- Salt and pepper to taste

Instructions:

1. Preheat your oven to 375°F (190°C). Line a baking sheet with parchment paper or lightly grease it with olive oil.
2. In a food processor, combine the drained chickpeas, chopped onion, minced garlic, chopped parsley, chopped cilantro, olive oil, lemon juice, ground cumin,

ground coriander, baking powder, salt, and pepper. Pulse until the mixture is well combined but still slightly chunky.
3. If the mixture seems too wet, you can add breadcrumbs to help bind it together. Start with 1/4 cup breadcrumbs and add more as needed until the mixture holds its shape when formed into balls.
4. Using your hands, shape the falafel mixture into small balls or patties and place them on the prepared baking sheet.
5. Bake the falafel in the preheated oven for 20-25 minutes, flipping halfway through baking, until golden brown and crispy on the outside.
6. While the falafel is baking, prepare the tzatziki sauce. In a small bowl, combine Greek yogurt, grated cucumber, minced garlic, fresh lemon juice, chopped dill, salt, and pepper. Stir until well combined.
7. Taste and adjust the seasoning of the tzatziki sauce, adding more salt, pepper, or lemon juice if needed.
8. Once the falafel is cooked, remove them from the oven and let them cool for a few minutes.
9. Serve the Baked Falafel hot with the Tzatziki Sauce on the side for dipping.
10. Enjoy your flavorful and satisfying Baked Falafel with Tzatziki Sauce!

These baked falafel are healthier than the traditional fried version, yet still packed with flavor and texture. They're perfect for serving as an appetizer, snack, or part of a Mediterranean-inspired meal.

Grilled Portobello Mushrooms with Balsamic Glaze

Ingredients:

- 4 large portobello mushrooms, stems removed
- 3 tablespoons balsamic vinegar
- 2 tablespoons olive oil
- 2 cloves garlic, minced
- 1 teaspoon dried thyme (or 1 tablespoon fresh thyme leaves)
- Salt and pepper to taste
- Fresh parsley, chopped, for garnish (optional)

For the Balsamic Glaze:

- 1/2 cup balsamic vinegar
- 2 tablespoons honey (or maple syrup for a vegan option)
- 1 teaspoon Dijon mustard

Instructions:

1. Preheat your grill to medium-high heat.
2. In a small bowl, whisk together balsamic vinegar, olive oil, minced garlic, dried thyme, salt, and pepper to make the marinade.
3. Brush both sides of the portobello mushrooms with the marinade, making sure they are evenly coated.
4. Place the mushrooms on the preheated grill, gill-side down. Grill for 4-5 minutes on each side, or until the mushrooms are tender and grill marks appear.
5. While the mushrooms are grilling, prepare the balsamic glaze. In a small saucepan, combine balsamic vinegar, honey (or maple syrup), and Dijon mustard. Bring to a simmer over medium heat.
6. Reduce the heat to low and simmer for 8-10 minutes, stirring occasionally, until the glaze is thickened and coats the back of a spoon.
7. Remove the grilled portobello mushrooms from the grill and transfer them to a serving platter.
8. Drizzle the balsamic glaze over the grilled mushrooms.
9. Garnish with chopped fresh parsley if desired.

10. Serve the Grilled Portobello Mushrooms with Balsamic Glaze hot as a delicious and elegant appetizer or side dish.
11. Enjoy your flavorful and satisfying grilled mushrooms with the sweet and tangy balsamic glaze!

These grilled portobello mushrooms are perfect for summer cookouts or as a meatless option for vegetarians and vegans. They're full of flavor and make a beautiful presentation on the dinner table.

Spicy Thai Coconut Curry with Vegetables

Ingredients:

- 1 tablespoon coconut oil (or vegetable oil)
- 1 onion, diced
- 2 cloves garlic, minced
- 1 tablespoon fresh ginger, grated
- 2 tablespoons Thai red curry paste
- 1 can (400ml) coconut milk
- 2 cups mixed vegetables (such as bell peppers, broccoli, carrots, snap peas)
- 1 cup tofu, diced (optional)
- 1 tablespoon soy sauce (or tamari for gluten-free)
- 1 tablespoon brown sugar (or coconut sugar)
- Juice of 1 lime
- Salt and pepper to taste
- Fresh cilantro, chopped, for garnish (optional)
- Cooked rice or noodles for serving

Instructions:

1. Heat coconut oil in a large skillet or wok over medium heat. Add diced onion, minced garlic, and grated ginger. Cook for 2-3 minutes until fragrant and softened.
2. Stir in Thai red curry paste and cook for another 1-2 minutes, stirring constantly.
3. Pour in the coconut milk and stir until the curry paste is fully incorporated into the milk.
4. Add mixed vegetables and diced tofu (if using) to the skillet. Stir to coat the vegetables and tofu with the curry sauce.
5. Cover the skillet and let the curry simmer for 8-10 minutes, or until the vegetables are tender and the flavors have melded together.
6. Stir in soy sauce (or tamari), brown sugar (or coconut sugar), and lime juice. Season with salt and pepper to taste.
7. Remove the skillet from heat and taste the curry, adjusting the seasoning if needed.
8. Serve the Spicy Thai Coconut Curry hot over cooked rice or noodles.
9. Garnish with chopped fresh cilantro if desired.

10. Enjoy your flavorful and aromatic Spicy Thai Coconut Curry with Vegetables!

This curry is packed with vibrant flavors and rich coconut creaminess. It's perfect for a cozy dinner at home or for entertaining guests. Feel free to customize the vegetables and protein according to your preference. It's also easily adaptable to be made vegan or gluten-free.

Broccoli and Cheddar Stuffed Chicken Breast

Ingredients:

- 4 boneless, skinless chicken breasts
- Salt and pepper to taste
- 1 cup broccoli florets, cooked and chopped
- 1 cup shredded cheddar cheese
- 2 cloves garlic, minced
- 1 tablespoon olive oil
- 1 teaspoon dried thyme (or 1 tablespoon fresh thyme leaves)
- 1/2 teaspoon paprika
- 1/4 teaspoon red pepper flakes (optional)
- Cooking twine or toothpicks

Instructions:

1. Preheat your oven to 375°F (190°C). Lightly grease a baking dish with olive oil or non-stick cooking spray.
2. Place each chicken breast between two sheets of plastic wrap or parchment paper. Use a meat mallet or rolling pin to pound the chicken breasts to an even thickness, about 1/2 inch thick. Season both sides of the chicken breasts with salt and pepper to taste.
3. In a mixing bowl, combine chopped broccoli florets, shredded cheddar cheese, minced garlic, olive oil, dried thyme, paprika, and red pepper flakes (if using). Mix until well combined.
4. Spoon the broccoli and cheddar mixture onto one half of each chicken breast, leaving a border around the edges. Fold the other half of the chicken breast over the filling to enclose it.
5. Secure the stuffed chicken breasts closed with cooking twine or toothpicks.
6. Place the stuffed chicken breasts in the prepared baking dish.
7. Bake in the preheated oven for 25-30 minutes, or until the chicken is cooked through and no longer pink in the center.
8. Remove the stuffed chicken breasts from the oven and let them rest for a few minutes before serving.
9. Serve the Broccoli and Cheddar Stuffed Chicken Breast hot as a delicious and satisfying meal!

10. Enjoy your flavorful and cheesy stuffed chicken breasts with a side of steamed vegetables, salad, or your favorite grain.

This dish is perfect for a weeknight dinner or a special occasion. The combination of tender chicken, savory broccoli, and melted cheddar cheese is sure to be a hit with your family and friends!

Turkey and Vegetable Meatloaf

Ingredients:

- 500g ground turkey
- 1 onion, finely chopped
- 2 cloves garlic, minced
- 1 carrot, grated
- 1 zucchini, grated
- 1/2 cup breadcrumbs (or oats for a gluten-free option)
- 1/4 cup ketchup
- 2 tablespoons Worcestershire sauce
- 1 tablespoon Dijon mustard
- 1 tablespoon fresh parsley, chopped
- 1 teaspoon dried oregano
- 1 teaspoon dried thyme
- 1/2 teaspoon paprika
- Salt and pepper to taste
- Olive oil for greasing

For the Glaze:

- 1/4 cup ketchup
- 2 tablespoons brown sugar
- 1 tablespoon apple cider vinegar

Instructions:

1. Preheat your oven to 375°F (190°C). Grease a loaf pan with olive oil and set aside.
2. In a large mixing bowl, combine ground turkey, chopped onion, minced garlic, grated carrot, grated zucchini, breadcrumbs, ketchup, Worcestershire sauce, Dijon mustard, chopped parsley, dried oregano, dried thyme, paprika, salt, and pepper. Mix until all ingredients are well combined.
3. Transfer the turkey mixture to the greased loaf pan and press it evenly into the pan.

4. In a small bowl, whisk together ketchup, brown sugar, and apple cider vinegar to make the glaze.
5. Spread the glaze evenly over the top of the meatloaf.
6. Bake the meatloaf in the preheated oven for 45-50 minutes, or until cooked through and the internal temperature reaches 165°F (75°C).
7. Once cooked, remove the meatloaf from the oven and let it rest for a few minutes before slicing.
8. Slice the Turkey and Vegetable Meatloaf and serve hot.
9. Enjoy your flavorful and nutritious meatloaf with your favorite side dishes, such as mashed potatoes, roasted vegetables, or a green salad.

This Turkey and Vegetable Meatloaf is packed with protein and loaded with veggies, making it a healthy and satisfying meal option. It's perfect for a cozy family dinner or for meal prep to enjoy throughout the week. Feel free to customize the recipe by adding other vegetables or herbs according to your taste preferences.

Cauliflower and Chickpea Curry

Ingredients:

- 1 tablespoon coconut oil or vegetable oil
- 1 onion, chopped
- 3 cloves garlic, minced
- 1 tablespoon fresh ginger, grated
- 1 cauliflower, cut into florets
- 1 can (400g) chickpeas, drained and rinsed
- 1 can (400ml) coconut milk
- 1 can (400g) diced tomatoes
- 2 tablespoons tomato paste
- 2 teaspoons curry powder
- 1 teaspoon ground turmeric
- 1 teaspoon ground cumin
- 1 teaspoon ground coriander
- 1/2 teaspoon red pepper flakes (optional)
- Salt and pepper to taste
- Fresh cilantro, chopped, for garnish (optional)
- Cooked rice or naan bread for serving

Instructions:

1. Heat coconut oil or vegetable oil in a large skillet or pot over medium heat.
2. Add chopped onion to the skillet and cook until softened, about 3-4 minutes.
3. Stir in minced garlic and grated ginger, and cook for another 1-2 minutes until fragrant.
4. Add cauliflower florets to the skillet and cook for 5-6 minutes, stirring occasionally, until lightly browned.
5. Stir in drained and rinsed chickpeas, diced tomatoes, tomato paste, curry powder, ground turmeric, ground cumin, ground coriander, and red pepper flakes (if using). Mix well to combine all the ingredients.
6. Pour in coconut milk and stir until everything is well combined. Season with salt and pepper to taste.
7. Bring the mixture to a simmer, then reduce the heat to low. Cover and let it simmer for 15-20 minutes, stirring occasionally, until the cauliflower is tender.

8. Taste and adjust the seasoning if needed.
9. Once the cauliflower is cooked and the curry has thickened slightly, remove the skillet from heat.
10. Serve the Cauliflower and Chickpea Curry hot over cooked rice or with naan bread.
11. Garnish with chopped fresh cilantro if desired.
12. Enjoy your flavorful and aromatic Cauliflower and Chickpea Curry!

This curry is packed with protein, fiber, and delicious flavors. It's perfect for a cozy dinner at home or for entertaining guests. Feel free to adjust the spices according to your taste preferences, and add more vegetables or protein if desired.

Lemon Garlic Roasted Chicken Thighs

Ingredients:

- 8 bone-in, skin-on chicken thighs
- 3 cloves garlic, minced
- Zest of 1 lemon
- Juice of 1 lemon
- 2 tablespoons olive oil
- 1 teaspoon dried thyme (or 1 tablespoon fresh thyme leaves)
- 1 teaspoon dried rosemary
- Salt and pepper to taste
- Lemon slices for garnish (optional)
- Fresh parsley, chopped, for garnish (optional)

Instructions:

1. Preheat your oven to 400°F (200°C). Line a baking sheet with parchment paper or aluminum foil for easy cleanup.
2. In a small bowl, combine minced garlic, lemon zest, lemon juice, olive oil, dried thyme, dried rosemary, salt, and pepper. Mix until well combined.
3. Place the chicken thighs on the prepared baking sheet, skin-side up.
4. Brush the lemon garlic mixture over the chicken thighs, making sure they are evenly coated.
5. Arrange lemon slices on top of the chicken thighs for extra flavor (optional).
6. Roast the chicken thighs in the preheated oven for 30-35 minutes, or until the skin is golden brown and crispy, and the internal temperature reaches 165°F (75°C).
7. Once cooked, remove the chicken thighs from the oven and let them rest for a few minutes.
8. Garnish with chopped fresh parsley if desired.
9. Serve the Lemon Garlic Roasted Chicken Thighs hot with your favorite side dishes, such as roasted vegetables, mashed potatoes, or a fresh salad.
10. Enjoy your flavorful and succulent Lemon Garlic Roasted Chicken Thighs!

This recipe is simple to make and yields tender and juicy chicken thighs with a burst of lemon and garlic flavor. It's perfect for a family dinner or for meal prep to enjoy throughout the week. Feel free to customize the recipe by adjusting the seasoning according to your taste preferences.

Baked Salmon with Dill Sauce

Ingredients:

For the Salmon:

- 4 salmon fillets (about 6 ounces each)
- 2 tablespoons olive oil
- Salt and pepper to taste
- 1 lemon, sliced (optional)

For the Dill Sauce:

- 1/2 cup Greek yogurt (or sour cream)
- 2 tablespoons mayonnaise
- 1 tablespoon lemon juice
- 1 tablespoon fresh dill, chopped (or 1 teaspoon dried dill)
- 1 clove garlic, minced
- Salt and pepper to taste

Instructions:

1. Preheat your oven to 375°F (190°C). Line a baking sheet with parchment paper or aluminum foil.
2. Place the salmon fillets on the prepared baking sheet. Drizzle olive oil over the salmon and season with salt and pepper to taste. If desired, place lemon slices on top of each salmon fillet.
3. Bake the salmon in the preheated oven for 12-15 minutes, or until the salmon is cooked through and flakes easily with a fork.
4. While the salmon is baking, prepare the dill sauce. In a small bowl, combine Greek yogurt (or sour cream), mayonnaise, lemon juice, chopped dill, minced garlic, salt, and pepper. Mix until well combined.
5. Taste the dill sauce and adjust the seasoning if needed, adding more salt, pepper, or lemon juice to taste.

6. Once the salmon is cooked, remove it from the oven and let it rest for a few minutes.
7. Serve the Baked Salmon hot with the Dill Sauce on the side for dipping or drizzling.
8. Enjoy your flavorful and tender Baked Salmon with Dill Sauce!

This dish is simple to prepare and bursting with fresh flavors. The creamy dill sauce pairs perfectly with the tender and flaky salmon. Serve the salmon with your favorite side dishes, such as roasted vegetables, steamed rice, or a fresh salad, for a complete and satisfying meal.

Mediterranean Quinoa Salad

Ingredients:

For the Salad:

- 1 cup quinoa, rinsed
- 2 cups water or vegetable broth
- 1 cup cherry tomatoes, halved
- 1 cucumber, diced
- 1/2 red onion, finely chopped
- 1/2 cup Kalamata olives, pitted and halved
- 1/4 cup crumbled feta cheese (optional)
- 1/4 cup fresh parsley, chopped
- 1/4 cup fresh mint, chopped (optional)
- Salt and pepper to taste

For the Dressing:

- 1/4 cup extra virgin olive oil
- 2 tablespoons lemon juice
- 1 clove garlic, minced
- 1 teaspoon dried oregano
- Salt and pepper to taste

Instructions:

1. In a medium saucepan, combine quinoa and water or vegetable broth. Bring to a boil, then reduce heat to low, cover, and simmer for 15-20 minutes, or until the quinoa is cooked and the liquid is absorbed. Remove from heat and let it cool.
2. In a large mixing bowl, combine the cooked quinoa, halved cherry tomatoes, diced cucumber, finely chopped red onion, halved Kalamata olives, crumbled feta cheese (if using), chopped fresh parsley, and chopped fresh mint (if using). Mix well to combine all the ingredients.

3. In a small bowl, whisk together extra virgin olive oil, lemon juice, minced garlic, dried oregano, salt, and pepper to make the dressing.
4. Pour the dressing over the quinoa salad and toss until everything is evenly coated in the dressing.
5. Taste and adjust the seasoning with more salt, pepper, or lemon juice if needed.
6. Cover the bowl with plastic wrap or transfer the salad to an airtight container. Refrigerate for at least 30 minutes to allow the flavors to meld together.
7. Before serving, give the Mediterranean Quinoa Salad a final toss.
8. Serve the salad chilled as a delicious and nutritious side dish or light meal.
9. Enjoy your flavorful and refreshing Mediterranean Quinoa Salad!

This salad is packed with protein, fiber, and vitamins, making it a healthy and satisfying option for lunch or dinner. It's also perfect for picnics, potlucks, or as a side dish for grilled meats or seafood. Feel free to customize the salad by adding other Mediterranean-inspired ingredients such as artichoke hearts, roasted red peppers, or sun-dried tomatoes.

Tofu and Vegetable Stir-Fry with Peanut Sauce

Ingredients:

For the Stir-Fry:

- 1 block (about 14 oz) firm tofu, pressed and cubed
- 2 tablespoons soy sauce (or tamari for gluten-free)
- 1 tablespoon sesame oil
- 1 tablespoon cornstarch
- 2 tablespoons vegetable oil, divided
- 2 cups broccoli florets
- 1 red bell pepper, thinly sliced
- 1 carrot, julienned
- 1 cup snap peas
- 3 cloves garlic, minced
- 1 tablespoon grated ginger
- Cooked rice or noodles for serving

For the Peanut Sauce:

- 1/4 cup natural peanut butter
- 2 tablespoons soy sauce (or tamari)
- 1 tablespoon maple syrup (or honey)
- 1 tablespoon rice vinegar
- 1 teaspoon sesame oil
- 1 clove garlic, minced
- 1 teaspoon grated ginger
- 2-4 tablespoons water, as needed

Instructions:

1. In a bowl, combine cubed tofu, soy sauce, sesame oil, and cornstarch. Toss gently to coat the tofu cubes evenly.

2. Heat 1 tablespoon of vegetable oil in a large skillet or wok over medium-high heat. Add the tofu cubes and cook until golden brown on all sides, about 5-7 minutes. Remove tofu from the skillet and set aside.
3. In the same skillet, heat the remaining tablespoon of vegetable oil. Add broccoli florets, sliced red bell pepper, julienned carrot, and snap peas. Stir-fry for 3-4 minutes, or until the vegetables are tender-crisp.
4. Add minced garlic and grated ginger to the skillet, and cook for another 1-2 minutes, stirring constantly until fragrant.
5. Return the cooked tofu to the skillet and toss with the vegetables to combine.
6. Meanwhile, prepare the peanut sauce. In a small bowl, whisk together peanut butter, soy sauce, maple syrup, rice vinegar, sesame oil, minced garlic, and grated ginger. Thin out the sauce with water, 1 tablespoon at a time, until desired consistency is reached.
7. Pour the peanut sauce over the tofu and vegetable mixture in the skillet. Stir well to coat everything in the sauce.
8. Cook for another 1-2 minutes, stirring constantly, until the sauce is heated through and the tofu and vegetables are evenly coated.
9. Remove the skillet from heat and serve the Tofu and Vegetable Stir-Fry hot over cooked rice or noodles.
10. Enjoy your flavorful and satisfying Tofu and Vegetable Stir-Fry with Peanut Sauce!

This dish is packed with protein, fiber, and delicious flavors. It's perfect for a quick and easy weeknight meal, and you can customize it by adding your favorite vegetables or adjusting the level of spiciness in the peanut sauce. Feel free to garnish with chopped peanuts, sesame seeds, or fresh cilantro for extra flavor and texture.

Baked Cod with Herbed Crust

Ingredients:

- 4 cod fillets (about 6 ounces each)
- 2 tablespoons olive oil
- 1 tablespoon lemon juice
- Salt and pepper to taste

For the Herbed Crust:

- 1/2 cup breadcrumbs (or panko breadcrumbs for a crispier crust)
- 2 tablespoons grated Parmesan cheese
- 1 tablespoon fresh parsley, chopped
- 1 tablespoon fresh dill, chopped
- 1 tablespoon fresh chives, chopped
- 1 teaspoon lemon zest
- 1 clove garlic, minced
- 2 tablespoons melted butter or olive oil

Instructions:

1. Preheat your oven to 400°F (200°C). Grease a baking dish with olive oil or non-stick cooking spray.
2. In a small bowl, combine olive oil and lemon juice. Brush the mixture over both sides of the cod fillets. Season with salt and pepper to taste.
3. In another bowl, combine breadcrumbs, grated Parmesan cheese, chopped parsley, chopped dill, chopped chives, lemon zest, and minced garlic. Mix well to combine.
4. Dip each cod fillet into the breadcrumb mixture, pressing gently to adhere the crumbs to the fish.
5. Place the breaded cod fillets in the prepared baking dish.
6. Drizzle melted butter or olive oil over the top of each cod fillet.
7. Bake in the preheated oven for 12-15 minutes, or until the cod is cooked through and flakes easily with a fork.
8. If desired, broil for an additional 1-2 minutes to brown the crust.

9. Remove the baked cod from the oven and let it rest for a few minutes before serving.
10. Serve the Baked Cod with Herbed Crust hot with your favorite side dishes, such as roasted vegetables, steamed rice, or a fresh salad.
11. Enjoy your flavorful and tender Baked Cod with Herbed Crust!

This dish is simple to prepare and bursting with fresh flavors from the herbs and lemon zest. The crunchy herbed crust adds texture and depth of flavor to the delicate cod fillets. It's perfect for a light and healthy dinner that's quick enough for busy weeknights but elegant enough for special occasions.

Turkey and White Bean Soup

Ingredients:

- 2 tablespoons olive oil
- 1 onion, chopped
- 2 carrots, diced
- 2 celery stalks, diced
- 3 cloves garlic, minced
- 1 teaspoon dried thyme
- 1 teaspoon dried rosemary
- 1 bay leaf
- Salt and pepper to taste
- 4 cups low-sodium chicken or turkey broth
- 2 cups cooked turkey, shredded or diced
- 2 cans (15 oz each) white beans (such as cannellini or Great Northern), drained and rinsed
- 1 cup frozen green beans
- 1/4 cup chopped fresh parsley
- 2 tablespoons lemon juice
- Grated Parmesan cheese for serving (optional)

Instructions:

1. In a large pot or Dutch oven, heat olive oil over medium heat. Add chopped onion, diced carrots, and diced celery. Cook, stirring occasionally, for about 5-7 minutes until vegetables are softened.
2. Add minced garlic, dried thyme, dried rosemary, bay leaf, salt, and pepper to the pot. Cook for another 1-2 minutes until fragrant.
3. Pour in chicken or turkey broth and bring the mixture to a boil. Once boiling, reduce the heat to low and let it simmer for about 10 minutes to allow the flavors to meld together.
4. Add shredded or diced cooked turkey, drained and rinsed white beans, and frozen green beans to the pot. Stir well to combine.
5. Let the soup simmer for another 10-15 minutes, stirring occasionally, until the turkey is heated through and the vegetables are tender.
6. Remove the bay leaf from the soup and discard.

7. Stir in chopped fresh parsley and lemon juice. Taste and adjust the seasoning with more salt, pepper, or lemon juice if needed.
8. Ladle the Turkey and White Bean Soup into bowls and serve hot.
9. Optionally, sprinkle grated Parmesan cheese over each serving before serving.
10. Enjoy your comforting and nourishing Turkey and White Bean Soup!

This soup is perfect for using up leftover turkey from holiday dinners, but you can also use rotisserie chicken or cooked turkey breast. It's hearty, flavorful, and packed with protein and fiber from the turkey and white beans. Serve it with crusty bread or a side salad for a complete and satisfying meal.

Grilled Vegetable Quesadillas

Ingredients:

- 4 large flour tortillas
- 1 red bell pepper, thinly sliced
- 1 yellow bell pepper, thinly sliced
- 1 green bell pepper, thinly sliced
- 1 red onion, thinly sliced
- 1 zucchini, thinly sliced
- 1 cup shredded cheese (cheddar, Monterey Jack, or a Mexican blend)
- Olive oil
- Salt and pepper to taste
- Optional toppings: salsa, sour cream, guacamole

Instructions:

1. Preheat your grill or grill pan over medium-high heat.
2. In a large bowl, toss the sliced bell peppers, red onion, and zucchini with a drizzle of olive oil until evenly coated. Season with salt and pepper to taste.
3. Place the vegetables on the grill in a single layer. Grill for 3-4 minutes per side, or until they are tender and have grill marks. Remove from the grill and set aside.
4. Lay out two tortillas on a clean surface. Sprinkle each tortilla with shredded cheese.
5. Divide the grilled vegetables evenly between the two tortillas, spreading them out over the cheese.
6. Top each tortilla with another tortilla to create a quesadilla.
7. Heat a large skillet or grill pan over medium heat. Carefully transfer one quesadilla to the skillet and cook for 2-3 minutes on each side, or until the tortillas are golden brown and the cheese is melted. Repeat with the second quesadilla.
8. Once both quesadillas are cooked, remove them from the skillet and let them cool for a minute before slicing into wedges.
9. Serve the Grilled Vegetable Quesadillas hot with your favorite toppings such as salsa, sour cream, or guacamole.
10. Enjoy your delicious and flavorful Grilled Vegetable Quesadillas!

These quesadillas are a great way to enjoy the smoky flavor of grilled vegetables and the gooey goodness of melted cheese. They're versatile, so feel free to customize them with your favorite vegetables or add some cooked chicken or beans for extra protein. They're perfect for a quick and easy meal that the whole family will love!

Lemon Herb Baked Tilapia

Ingredients:

- 4 tilapia fillets (about 6 ounces each)
- 2 tablespoons olive oil
- 2 tablespoons lemon juice
- 2 cloves garlic, minced
- 1 tablespoon fresh parsley, chopped
- 1 tablespoon fresh dill, chopped
- 1 tablespoon fresh chives, chopped
- 1 teaspoon lemon zest
- Salt and pepper to taste
- Lemon slices for garnish (optional)

Instructions:

1. Preheat your oven to 400°F (200°C). Grease a baking dish with olive oil or non-stick cooking spray.
2. In a small bowl, whisk together olive oil, lemon juice, minced garlic, chopped parsley, chopped dill, chopped chives, lemon zest, salt, and pepper.
3. Place the tilapia fillets in the prepared baking dish in a single layer.
4. Pour the lemon herb mixture over the tilapia fillets, making sure they are evenly coated.
5. If desired, place lemon slices on top of each tilapia fillet for extra flavor.
6. Bake the tilapia in the preheated oven for 12-15 minutes, or until the fish is opaque and flakes easily with a fork.
7. Once cooked, remove the tilapia from the oven and let it rest for a few minutes before serving.
8. Serve the Lemon Herb Baked Tilapia hot with your favorite side dishes, such as steamed vegetables, rice, or quinoa.
9. Enjoy your flavorful and tender Lemon Herb Baked Tilapia!

This dish is quick and easy to prepare, making it perfect for busy weeknights. The combination of fresh herbs, lemon, and garlic adds brightness and depth of flavor to the mild tilapia fillets. Serve it as a light and healthy meal that the whole family will love!

Lentil and Vegetable Shepherd's Pie

Ingredients:

For the Filling:

- 1 cup dry green or brown lentils, rinsed
- 2 cups vegetable broth
- 1 tablespoon olive oil
- 1 onion, chopped
- 2 carrots, diced
- 2 celery stalks, diced
- 2 cloves garlic, minced
- 1 teaspoon dried thyme
- 1 teaspoon dried rosemary
- 1 teaspoon paprika
- Salt and pepper to taste
- 1 cup frozen peas
- 1 cup frozen corn
- 2 tablespoons tomato paste
- 2 tablespoons soy sauce or tamari (for umami flavor)
- 1 tablespoon Worcestershire sauce (optional)

For the Mashed Potato Topping:

- 2 pounds potatoes (such as russet or Yukon gold), peeled and diced
- 1/4 cup unsalted butter or vegan butter
- 1/2 cup milk or non-dairy milk
- Salt and pepper to taste

Instructions:

1. Preheat your oven to 375°F (190°C).

2. In a medium saucepan, combine rinsed lentils and vegetable broth. Bring to a boil, then reduce heat to low, cover, and simmer for 20-25 minutes, or until the lentils are tender and most of the liquid is absorbed.
3. While the lentils are cooking, prepare the mashed potato topping. Place diced potatoes in a large pot and cover with water. Bring to a boil, then reduce heat to medium-low and simmer for 15-20 minutes, or until the potatoes are fork-tender. Drain the potatoes and return them to the pot.
4. Add butter and milk to the pot with the cooked potatoes. Mash with a potato masher or fork until smooth and creamy. Season with salt and pepper to taste. Set aside.
5. In a large skillet, heat olive oil over medium heat. Add chopped onion, diced carrots, and diced celery. Cook, stirring occasionally, for about 5-7 minutes until the vegetables are softened.
6. Add minced garlic, dried thyme, dried rosemary, paprika, salt, and pepper to the skillet. Cook for another 1-2 minutes until fragrant.
7. Stir in frozen peas and frozen corn. Cook for 2-3 minutes until the vegetables are heated through.
8. Add cooked lentils, tomato paste, soy sauce (or tamari), and Worcestershire sauce (if using) to the skillet. Mix well to combine all the ingredients.
9. Cook for another 2-3 minutes, stirring occasionally, until the filling is heated through and well combined.
10. Transfer the lentil and vegetable filling to a 9x13 inch baking dish or individual ramekins, spreading it out evenly.
11. Spread the mashed potato topping over the lentil and vegetable filling, smoothing it out with a spatula.
12. Bake in the preheated oven for 25-30 minutes, or until the mashed potato topping is lightly golden brown and the filling is bubbly around the edges.
13. Remove the Shepherd's Pie from the oven and let it cool for a few minutes before serving.
14. Serve the Lentil and Vegetable Shepherd's Pie hot as a comforting and satisfying meal!

This hearty and wholesome dish is packed with protein, fiber, and delicious flavors from the lentils, vegetables, and creamy mashed potato topping. It's perfect for a cozy family dinner or for meal prep to enjoy throughout the week. Feel free to customize the recipe by adding your favorite herbs, spices, or vegetables to suit your taste preferences.

Baked Chicken with Rosemary and Garlic

Ingredients:

- 4 bone-in, skin-on chicken breasts or thighs
- 2 tablespoons olive oil
- 4 cloves garlic, minced
- 2 tablespoons fresh rosemary leaves, chopped (or 2 teaspoons dried rosemary)
- Salt and pepper to taste
- 1 lemon, sliced (optional)

Instructions:

1. Preheat your oven to 400°F (200°C). Grease a baking dish large enough to hold the chicken pieces in a single layer.
2. In a small bowl, mix together olive oil, minced garlic, and chopped rosemary.
3. Place the chicken pieces in the prepared baking dish. Season them generously with salt and pepper.
4. Drizzle the olive oil, garlic, and rosemary mixture over the chicken pieces, spreading it evenly to coat each piece.
5. If using lemon slices, place them on top of the chicken pieces for extra flavor.
6. Bake the chicken in the preheated oven for 30-35 minutes, or until the chicken is golden brown and cooked through. The internal temperature should reach 165°F (75°C) for chicken breasts or 175°F (80°C) for chicken thighs.
7. Once cooked, remove the chicken from the oven and let it rest for a few minutes before serving.
8. Serve the Baked Chicken with Rosemary and Garlic hot with your favorite side dishes, such as roasted vegetables, mashed potatoes, or a fresh salad.
9. Enjoy your flavorful and tender Baked Chicken with Rosemary and Garlic!

This dish is simple to make yet full of robust flavors from the garlic and rosemary. The chicken turns out juicy and succulent with a crispy skin, making it perfect for a comforting and satisfying meal. Feel free to customize the recipe by adjusting the amount of garlic and rosemary according to your taste preferences.

Spaghetti Squash with Marinara Sauce

Ingredients:

- 1 medium spaghetti squash
- 2 cups marinara sauce (store-bought or homemade)
- Olive oil
- Salt and pepper to taste
- Fresh basil leaves for garnish (optional)
- Grated Parmesan cheese for garnish (optional)

Instructions:

1. Preheat your oven to 400°F (200°C).
2. Cut the spaghetti squash in half lengthwise and scoop out the seeds with a spoon.
3. Drizzle the cut sides of the squash with olive oil and season with salt and pepper.
4. Place the squash halves cut-side down on a baking sheet lined with parchment paper.
5. Roast the squash in the preheated oven for 40-50 minutes, or until the flesh is tender and easily pierced with a fork.
6. Once the squash is cooked, remove it from the oven and let it cool slightly.
7. Using a fork, scrape the flesh of the squash to create spaghetti-like strands.
8. Heat the marinara sauce in a saucepan over medium heat until warmed through.
9. Divide the spaghetti squash strands among serving plates or bowls.
10. Top each serving of spaghetti squash with marinara sauce.
11. Garnish with fresh basil leaves and grated Parmesan cheese, if desired.
12. Serve the Spaghetti Squash with Marinara Sauce hot and enjoy!

This dish is a healthy and satisfying alternative to traditional pasta. The spaghetti squash provides a low-carb and nutrient-rich base for the marinara sauce, which is packed with flavor. Feel free to add your favorite toppings or additional vegetables to customize the dish to your liking. It's perfect for a light and delicious meal any day of the week!

Turkey and Vegetable Skillet Hash

Ingredients:

- 1 lb ground turkey
- 2 tablespoons olive oil
- 1 onion, diced
- 2 cloves garlic, minced
- 2 bell peppers (any color), diced
- 2 medium potatoes, diced into small cubes
- 1 teaspoon paprika
- 1/2 teaspoon dried thyme
- Salt and pepper to taste
- 2 cups baby spinach leaves
- Optional toppings: chopped green onions, fresh parsley, hot sauce

Instructions:

1. Heat olive oil in a large skillet over medium heat. Add diced onion and minced garlic, and cook until softened and fragrant, about 2-3 minutes.
2. Add ground turkey to the skillet and cook, breaking it apart with a spoon, until it's browned and cooked through, about 5-7 minutes.
3. Add diced bell peppers and potatoes to the skillet. Season with paprika, dried thyme, salt, and pepper. Stir well to combine all the ingredients.
4. Cook the mixture, stirring occasionally, until the potatoes are tender and golden brown, about 10-12 minutes.
5. Once the potatoes are cooked, add baby spinach leaves to the skillet. Stir until the spinach is wilted and combined with the rest of the ingredients, about 2-3 minutes.
6. Taste the hash and adjust the seasoning with more salt and pepper if needed.
7. Remove the skillet from the heat and let the hash rest for a few minutes before serving.
8. Serve the Turkey and Vegetable Skillet Hash hot, topped with chopped green onions, fresh parsley, and hot sauce if desired.
9. Enjoy your hearty and flavorful Turkey and Vegetable Skillet Hash!

This dish is perfect for a satisfying breakfast, brunch, or dinner. It's packed with protein and loaded with colorful vegetables, making it both nutritious and delicious. Feel free to customize the recipe by adding other vegetables such as zucchini, mushrooms, or cherry tomatoes. It's a versatile dish that's sure to become a favorite in your meal rotation!